Creative Visualization and Self Hypnosis

How to Use the Power of Your Imagination and Self Hypnosis to Create What You Want in Life

By Tim Reid

Copyright 2014 by Tim Reid. Published by Make Profits Easy LLC

Profitsdaily123@aol.com

facebook.com/MakeProfitsEasy

Table of Contents

Introduction 5

Chapter 1: What is Creative Visualization? 8

Chapter 2: The Benefits of Creative Visualization 16

Chapter 3: Strategies for Effective Visualization 33

Chapter 4: What is Self Hypnosis? 65

Chapter 5: The Benefits of Self-Hypnosis 70

Chapter 6: Strategies for Effective Self Hypnosis 80

Conclusion 88

Introduction

Your mind is a powerful muscle that many people unfortunately do not utilize enough. There is a common misconception that our brain just does what it does automatically and we don't really have any control over it. But this is simply not true. Our mind is extremely powerful and, fortunately, many theorists have realized this power and developed strategies for exercising and actually using that power.

In this book you will learn about two of those strategies: creative visualization and self hypnosis. The former is a method by which you can control your life and the external world which surrounds you, drawing everything you want toward you and pushing all negativity away. The latter is a means by which you can retrain your own mind and body to change your habits, improve certain skills, or otherwise improve yourself as a human being.

Used together, you will be able to become who you want to be and have the life that you have always dreamed of—all using the magnificent power of your very own mind. Both take training and commitment in order to achieve the full effects but luckily, training methods and exercise techniques have already been developed to help you do just that.

All you need to do is determine exactly what you want to become and exactly how you want your life to be and then train your mind. Practice, practice, practice! This book is a comprehensive guide to everything you will need to know before you begin honing your mind's energy.

In the following chapters, you will learn:

- What creative visualization is
- How it works
- The science behind creative visualization
- What creative visualization can be used for

- How it can benefit you
- The techniques for effectively practicing creative visualization
- Methods for strengthening your mind
- What self hypnosis is
- How it works
- The science behind self hypnosis
- What self hypnosis can be used for
- How it can benefit you
- Techniques for practicing self hypnosis effectively
- Methods for improving your ability to conduct self hypnosis

So start reading and get ready to watch yourself and your life transform before your very eyes, using nothing more than the mental energy already contained within you!

Chapter 1: What is Creative Visualization?

Creative visualization is a method for achieving your dreams and making your life exactly what you want it to be. It requires intense, focused thought on your specific goals (visualization) in order to make those goals manifest themselves in your life (creative).

The theory behind creative visualization's effectiveness is known as the law of attraction which is the theory that like attracts like—a common characteristic of all energy in the universe. Essentially, there are many different forms of energy and one form of energy will attract similar forms to itself. Our thoughts, as with all forces in the universe, are made up of energy. That is, what you think or visualize is a form of energy that will attract similar forms of energy to you.

This gives your mind a very powerful ability that many unwittingly let go to waste, or worse, let it work against them. Many people think negatively and believe that nothing good can happen to them. These negative thoughts emit negative energy into the universe which then attracts negative energy to you. Therefore, if you *think* nothing good will happen to you, then you will be right because the negative energy from that sort of thinking is causing negative energy in the universe to come into your life.

On the other hand, if you think positively and believe that good things will happen to you in the future, then you will also be right. Just as your negative thoughts had been attracting negativity; your positive thoughts attract positivity.

Creative visualization, then, is the means by which you train your mind to focus all of its powerful mental energy into manifesting positive things in your life. The techniques used can help eliminate harmful negative thoughts and maximize the power of your positive thoughts.

Theories like that of creative visualization have been around for centuries. In England, as early as the 19th century, Thomas Troward wrote about how human thoughts precede forms. That is, pure raw energy exists before it takes shape as a specific form of matter. He also wrote that the energy of our thoughts, when allowed to continue without interruption into the universe, can and *will* attract all the conditions and materials you need to manifest your thoughts into their physical, material form.

Since Troward, many other thinkers have taken his theories further by defining specific and functional techniques for effectively channeling this mental energy in order to accomplish our goals.

The Science behind Creative Visualization

To better understand what you are doing when you visualize, you should have a basic understanding of the science behind it. Pure energy without material form is essentially a vibration. Your thoughts, then, are best understood as vibrations which you emit into the universe. The universe, then, will respond by returning a similar vibration back toward you. Sending out positive energy about what you would like to achieve will cause the universe to respond by sending back both the conditions and the material you will need to actually achieve it.

Let's use an example: say you would like an abundance of wealth so that you don't have to worry about financial security anymore. Visualizing yourself with that wealth and financial security will send out positive vibrations. The universe will then respond with similar vibrations. This could take many forms from an opportunity to get a promotion at work; a family inheritance; a better job offer; or a number of other possibilities.

One of the tenants of quantum mechanics is that observation affects outcome. That is to say, when a scientist conducts an experiment, the simple act of observing the phenomena will affect the results he or she sees. In a sense, scientists are observing what they want to observe. This is just a fraction of the full power of the human mind to change the external world in which we live.

Through quantum mechanics we have also learned about another phenomenon known as "quantum entanglement." Quantum entanglement argues that when two objects in the universe interact once, they remain connected with each other continuously even if they drift far apart. This speaks to the deeply rooted interconnectedness between humans and the rest of the universe—right down to the atomic level.

Due to the process of quantum entanglement, the entire universe is now interconnected and has been in this state of interconnection since the time of the big bang. The reason that everything is interconnected is because before the Big Bang, all the matter and energy in the entire universe was compacted into a singularity. At this point all matter and energy came into contact with each other and has remained connected ever since.

Therefore, the mental energy in our mind is interconnected with *everything* in the universe. This means that as your thoughts—whether positive or negative—vibrate outwards, they will eventually affect absolutely everything else that is in the universe.

Controlling and magnifying that mental energy through creative visualization, then, is an extremely powerful and useful skill. However, it is easier said than done. The universe, just like your mind, is exceedingly sensitive to even the most subtle of vibrations. This means that even the slightest hint of doubt or negativity in your mind will be sent out into the universe along with the rest of your attempts to creatively visualize positively. These subtle negative vibrations may not entirely overpower your positive thoughts but they will act as a serious ball and chain, preventing your creative visualization from working as effectively as it could be.

Because of the universe's sensitivity to all forms of energy, it will take time and effort for you to effectively master the techniques of creative visualization so that you can harness the full power of your mind. You cannot simply make the decision today to think positively and then suddenly eliminate all negative thoughts and have what you dreamed of by the same time tomorrow.

You have to practice and train. You have to focus your mental energy into these positive vibrations every single day. The more you do this, however, the easier it will become. Eventually, you will only think positively and all negative thoughts will have disappeared. But allow yourself the time to really train and exercise your mental energy before you tell yourself it's not going to work.

In chapter 3 of this book, you will learn about the specific techniques involved in creative visualization as well as other methods you can use to exercise and strengthen your mental energy. First, though, let's learn more about what exactly you can do with creative visualization and what its benefits are.

Chapter 2: The Benefits of Creative Visualization

There are many benefits and upsides to practicing creative visualization. Below is a list of just a few of them:

- It's something you already do anyway: your mind is already visualizing all the time. The only difference is that you have not yet trained your mind to use visualization to the best of your ability and in order to accomplish exactly what you want. You can think of it as the difference between just eating and eating healthy. Everybody can and does eat every single day. But only some people have mastered an understanding of nutrition so that they can eat the right balance of food in order to gain the many wonderful benefits of a healthy diet.

Furthermore, there is a huge difference between eating nothing but junk food and eating a healthy, balanced diet. With junk food, you might feel temporarily relieved but in the long term, you feel sluggish, lazy, and develop all sorts of health problems. This is the same with visualization. Without training, your mind is full of "junk" thoughts, or negative thoughts that make you feel bad about yourself, lazy, or even depressed. With training, however, visualization will energize you, empower you, and make you feel as if you are on top of the world.

- It produces alpha brain waves: at the biological level, creative visualization is producing alpha waves in your brain. Your brain produces all sorts of waves depending on its current state. Alpha waves are produced when your mind is relaxed and at ease. These waves can lower blood pressure, decrease anxiety, and regulate your heart beat to decrease your risk for heart attack.

That means that creative visualization can have immediate benefits even before what you have visualized has manifested itself in your life! The more you practice creative visualization, the more quickly your mind is able to shift into alpha waves. Soon, you will have the mental strength to immediately put yourself into a relaxed and calm state. With that sort of ability, you can eliminate stress and feelings of being overwhelmed from your life almost entirely!

- It helps control your subconscious: our subconscious is responsible for all of our desires, dreams, and impulsive behaviors. Creative visualization gives you full control of your entire mind, including your subconscious. With the ability to control it, you would have a deeper understanding of yourself and who you really are.

You would also be able to get in touch with your real desires and aspirations. And more than that, you would know *why* you desire those things. The ability to control your impulses will help you stay in touch with your emotions so that you can understand them and make sure that they don't overrule your reason.

- It's really fun: even though it takes practice, creative visualization is a lot of fun—even at the beginning. You are taking the time to thoroughly visualize in vivid detail every aspect of your dream life. And with creative visualization, you start to feel how you would feel if that life were your reality right now. It's a pretty great feeling.

  So if you find yourself bored in line at the grocery store or waiting at the doctor's office, instead of being bored, you can use that time to enjoy some creative visualization. It's sort of like a super-powered version of day dreaming!

- It boosts your confidence: the secret to confidence is knowing what you want and knowing that you have the power to get it. With creative visualization, you have both of those down. You are visualizing every little detail of what you want (knowing absolutely everything about it) and you know that as your mind gets stronger, your visualizations become more and more powerful so you are already on the way to getting it. This will build your confidence up more and more. And a healthy level of confidence is going to carry you a long way.

- It increases the number of opportunities you'll have: this happens for two reasons. First of all, creative visualization is actually attracting opportunities to you through the power of your positive mental vibrations. Secondly, the more you practice creative visualization, the better you will become at *recognizing* those opportunities because you will better be able to identify how everything is interconnected and what the best way is to bring you closer to what you want.

Finally, your increased confidence will also open up more opportunities for you. People are naturally drawn to confidence and as you grow to have more confidence in yourself, others will start to have more confidence in you and be willing to take chances on you.

- It builds new neural pathways: creative visualization can actually alter the structure of your brain so that you are better prepared for success. Research has shown that vividly imagining yourself doing something actually exercises the same parts of the brain as actually doing it. Therefore, if you want to, say, be an athlete, visualizing yourself playing the sport will actually train your brain in how to play. Then, when you are training for the sport, you will already have a mental advantage. Think of creative visualization as a sort of "mental rehearsal" for real world success!

- It decreases anxiety and depression: while it is boosting your confidence, it will also be decreasing your anxiety in depression. This is due to a variety of factors including the fact that creative visualization produces alpha brain waves which you have already read about above. These brain waves will decrease your anxiety and help you to relax. The increased confidence and empowered feeling you get from creative visualization will also help to decrease depression and prevent it from coming again.

- It improves your cognitive skills: creative visualization really is mental exercise. It improves important cognitive skills like focus and concentration which will help you perform better at work, in your studies, or while playing sports. These are important skills that you need in order to better take advantage of the opportunities that are soon going to be presenting themselves to you as you get better and better at creative visualization.

  So, even as you are still training and have not yet fully mastered the techniques, you will already be sharpening these important skills. Combine those with the "mental rehearsal" and you will be fully 100% prepared to take charge of every opportunity that comes your way and ensure that you do reach the success that you desire.

- It helps you think more constructively: creative visualization changes the way that you think and the way that you approach life. Rather than encountering a problem and having negative thoughts about how horrible the problem is or how there is nothing you can do about it, you will immediately start visualizing your life in the future when that problem is resolved. Then you can work backwards from there and imagine the potential steps you took to overcome the problem.

In this way, you are actually thinking about solutions rather than worrying about problems. And because your anxiety will be lower throughout this whole process, you will be even more capable of finding a solution because your mind won't be overstressed.

- It is a source of inspiration: as mentioned earlier, creative visualization changes the structure of your brain. With these new neural pathways, you will actually be more capable of making new connections and coming up with new ideas that actually were not even possible before because you simply lacked the neural pathways for those ideas.

Furthermore, as your creative visualizations become more and more detailed, you are strengthening your imagination and your imagination plays a huge role in inspiration and the creation of new and innovative ideas. This will help you to create your very own opportunities to achieve success. Now, how's that for mental power?

Now that you have an idea of how creative visualization benefits your mind, it's time to look at the sort of things that creative visualization can help you achieve. The following list is, by no means, comprehensive. The uses of creative visualization are limited only by your imagination.

However, when you have never done it before, it can be hard to think of exactly what you should be using it for. There are also some guidelines for what you should be trying to creatively visualize. So this short list is only meant to inspire you to think more about what *you* specifically want and how to come up with and construct a goal on which you can most effectively use creative visualization:

- Financial Security: this is one of the most common things people use creative visualization to accomplish. The actor Jim Carrey, for example, used creative visualization to become a millionaire. In 1987, before he had achieved his fame, he wrote a check for $10 million to himself and dated it for Thanksgiving of 1995. By the end of 1994, he had signed a movie contract which earned him $10 million!

    Whether you want to earn millions or just to have enough to live comfortably without having to stress about how you'll pay the bills, creative visualization is the way to get there. However, you need to follow some general guidelines. Rather than saying "I want to be rich," figure out the specifics.

Jim Carrey didn't write a check for "being rich," he put the specific amount of $10 million. He even noted "for acting services rendered" on the check. This shows that he was visualizing exactly how much he hoped to earn, *how* he hoped to earn it, and when he hoped to earn it by (1995).

Make sure to include these sorts of details and more in your own creative visualization. The more detailed your visualization is, the more specific the form of energy you are sending out to the universe will be. Because like attracts like, you want to make sure that your positive energy is as detailed and unique as possible so that it can attract exactly what you need to make your creative visualization a reality.

- Success at Work: another popular use of creative visualization is to find greater success in your career. You can visualize a promotion, a pay raise, an entirely new job, opening your own business, saving enough to retire early, or anything else that you desire. Just remember that you need to be as specific as possible.

If you want a raise, how much of a raise do you want? If you want a promotion, what position would you like to be promoted to? What are the responsibilities and skills required of that position? If you want to open your own business, visualize yourself already leading that business to success.

What is your product or service? How many employees do you have to start? What are their specific responsibilities?

What are your responsibilities as owner and leader of your staff? If you would like to save enough to retire early or to retire more comfortably, visualize exactly how much you need to save; what your lifestyle will be like when you retire; what options you would like to have for building your retirement. Do you want to build it up only through savings or through a combination of savings and investing? As mentioned above, the more details you can add to your creative visualization, the clearer it will be to you and the clearer it will be to the universe.

- Success in Love: you can also use creative visualization to find success in love. You can visualize yourself meeting your soul mate or restoring your marriage which might be on the rocks right now. You can even visualize getting a divorce if you feel that this is what you truly want. Or it can be something as minor as visualizing the perfect Valentine's day with your loved one.

It could also be a broader type of success such as forming a happy family or it could be more specific such as being more skilled in the bedroom. Whatever it is that you desire, just remember to always be as specific as possible. Really visualize yourself having already achieved exactly what you want. Visualize yourself with your soul mate or in a happy marriage. Fill in the specific details such as what sort of qualities your soul mate has, or what it looks like to you to have a happy marriage. The more detailed your visualization, the better you can understand yourself what you want. This can help you better understand how to actually make it a reality.

- Success in Education: you can even use creative visualization to be better in your studies. Visualize getting into your first choice college or visualize yourself passing that important final exam. Just remember to be as specific as possible and really visualize every single little detail that forms part of what you want. The more detailed your idea is, the more accurate the physical manifestation of it will be.

- Specific Objects: creative visualization doesn't just have to be about success, wealth, and more general happenings. You can use it for everyday things, too. For example, if you want a new car, visualize the perfect car for you. If you need new clothes, visualize yourself looking amazing in a new outfit. What does that outfit look like?

  Using creative visualization for these sort of things is also a good idea because it will strengthen your mental power and give you an opportunity to practice the techniques on smaller, easier things. You can also use creative visualization for more than one thing at a time. However, don't overcrowd your mind.

Having one or two different creative visualizations that you are working on is perfectly manageable as long as you make sure to give time to focus on each rather than switching back and forth in one creative visualization session.

Chapter 3: Strategies for Effective Visualization

In order to use creative visualization effectively, you need to use a few different techniques. In this chapter, you will learn about those techniques as well as some methods for exercising your mental energy and even some common mistakes that you can avoid in order to make sure that you are not holding back your mind's power in any way.

Steps for Creative Visualization

By following these easy steps every day, you can visualize effectively and start making your dreams come true!

1. Know what you want: what you truly want is not as obvious as most people think it is. Your true desires are in your subconscious and all of your conscious wants are simply symbolic of these true desires. In order to use creative visualization effectively, you have to make

sure that you know exactly what kind of vibrations you are sending out there. Because even if you consciously are thinking "Money," your subconscious is sending out other (stronger) vibrations of what you actually want.

You probably can't just open up your subconscious right now and look inside. But what you can do is a little "pre-visualization." Think about your conscious desire. Let's say it is more money. What specific emotions would you feel if you had that money? Would it make you feel more secure? More confident? More successful?

The positive feeling that you would gain with more money is what you are really after. The money itself is actually completely irrelevant. So you will be more successful if you use creative visualization to visualize success, security, or whichever other feeling you are after. You can visualize some of the specific physical details (such as how you will look, how you will dress, where you will live, and so on) but know that these details could change in reality.

Your real world success could look different than how you imagined. This is why it is so important to tap into your subconscious and understand your true desires. While you may think something like money is the only way to feel those positive feelings, the universe could actually send you a number of other opportunities aside from money (such as a new baby or a more rewarding job, even though it does not pay much). These opportunities will allow you have that same sensation you would have with your conscious want but only if you are ready and able to recognize and seize it.

2. Pull out the negative thoughts by their roots: your negative thoughts are going to

be your biggest challenge with creative visualization. These thoughts will interfere with the positive vibrations you are sending out into the universe. They will cause more negative things to be attracted into your life which will set you on a downward spiral of feeling even more negative as a result of the increase in negative things. You have probably already experienced this negative spiral in some ways without realizing that it was actually your own thoughts that were attracting such negativity into your life.

In order to eliminate these harmful negative thoughts, you need to go back to your subconscious again. Just as your conscious wants are really just symbolic representations of your unconscious desire, so, too, are your negative thoughts symbolic representations of your unconscious fears. If you really want to permanently eliminate these thoughts, you have got to figure out what your unconscious fears are.

Just as you wouldn't just rip out the leaves and stem of a weed in your garden, you can't just rip out the conscious negative thought from your mind. It will only grow back—and this time even more vicious. You can use a similar process for understanding your unconscious fears as you did for your unconscious desires.

Start with your negative thought and then imagine how it would feel if that negativity had become a reality. If the negativity is already part of your reality, try to examine how you truly feel about the situation. Once you have identified what the unconscious fears are, you can start working on eliminating them. The methods you read about in the next section will help you do this.

3. Make affirmations: in the next section about mental exercises you are going to learn about how to do affirmations. Affirmations are an absolutely essential part of the creative visualization process so this is something you will really need to focus on. The stronger and more effective your affirmations are, the more effective the whole creative visualization process will be. This is because the process by which you do your affirmations allows them to enter down into your subconscious. There, they will be able to help you uproot your negative thoughts more easily and strengthen your unconscious desires.

Because your unconscious is sending out vibrations at all times (even while you are asleep and your conscious mind is resting), it is extremely important that you make the effort to strengthen your unconscious mind. That way, you can even use creative visualization in your sleep! The more positive vibrations you are able to send out into the universe, the more quickly you will be able to see your desires manifest into reality. These valuable hours you spend sleeping will maximize your visualization efforts. So make sure to pay very close attention to the instructions and tips about making effective affirmations in the next section of this chapter.

4. Repeat, repeat, repeat: what it all comes down to is practice. The key to mastering all of these techniques is simply to repeat them from day to day until it becomes second nature. Affirmations, for example, will not work if you just say it one time and then forget about it. You need to repeat it to yourself every single day, multiple times per day even. By the same logic, you cannot uproot all of your negative thoughts in just one go. It is

going to take repeated work, digging into your unconscious and pulling up all of your subconscious fears and anxieties that contribute to your negative thinking.

In fact, the whole process of creative visualization cannot just be done once. You must practice creative visualization every single day, the more positive vibrations you can send out into the universe, the stronger their collective effect will be. At face value, creative visualization sounds like an easy solution: just think about what you want and it will manifest itself.

But the fact is, it takes a lot of mental training in order to master the techniques and make sure that creative visualization works as it should. However, this dedication and hard work will more than pay off and leave you not only feeling happier but having the life you have always wanted.

5. Bring more positive energy into your life: one of the best ways to start building up your own positive energy is by bringing more of it into your life. You can take the initiative and get the ball rolling so that the universe has only to continue with the momentum you have already started.

There are number of different ways that you can bring more positive energy into your life. External energy (whether positive or negative) comes from the books you read, the tv shows you watch, the websites you surf, the people you associate with and so on. All of these different things are influencing your mind. So, if they are negative, it's again like eating junk food. You aren't feeding your mind anything it can use to construct positive creative visualizations. So try to cut the negative people out of your life and surround yourself with positive ones. Read books that you enjoy, watch tv shows that are positive or uplifting, visit websites that enrich your life (such as those that describe these techniques in more detail).

Doing this will give you more positive input for your mind to work with as you perfect the other techniques you are currently working on. It will make the process of eliminating your own internal negativity much easier as well.

6. Practice positive reflection: there is another part to creative visualization beyond using positive mental energy to attract the things you want into your life. This other part is positive reflection. This is the process by which, at the end of every day, you take some time reflect on what has happened.

With positive reflection, you are focusing exclusively on the positive developments. What are the good things that happened?

What progress have you made toward your goals (even if it was just one or two small steps)? If something negative happened, try to see if there are any hidden opportunities within it. Which positive opportunities have presented themselves to you today? Are there any that you overlooked but recognize now in this time of reflection?

Answering these questions each night will sharpen your mind and help you get better at seizing opportunities as they present themselves. It will also help strengthen your dedication and belief as you will be able to recognize the ways in which creative visualization has already started working for you.

This is an extremely important step because without this positive reflection, you may start to lose your motivation and you may be missing out on the very opportunities the universe is trying to present to you. The positive creative visualization is what will attract good things into your life but it is positive reflection that will enable you to actually recognize and take them.

Mental Exercises

When you first begin using creative visualization, your mind is completely untrained so it is not going to be as effective at using the techniques which you just read about above. For this reason, you need to do a certain amount of "reprogramming" so that your mind can build up its positive mental energy.

Doing the mental exercise methods described below on a daily basis while you practice the creative visualization techniques above. In addition to these exercises, you can use the techniques of self hypnosis which you will read about in detail in chapters 4-6 of this book. Self hypnosis is a means of "reprogramming" your mind so that you can be the person that you want to be.

Meditation

Mediation is a millennia old technique of mental strengthening. There are highly trained monks who are so skilled in meditation, they can control their own heartbeat. The more you practice meditation, the greater control you will have over your own mind and body. You will be able to fall asleep exactly when you want to, wake up when you want to without feeling groggy. You can even control your unconscious mind (which is notorious for being uncontrollable and usually requires intensive professional help from skilled therapists to help you even just manage it).

The purpose of meditation is neither to increase positive energy nor decrease negative energy. Rather, meditation will help you to increase the level of control you have over your mind so that *you* decide what sort of energy you put out. That is, meditation will sharpen your focus and allow you to fine tune exactly which vibrations you are sending out across the universe.

With that in mind, here are some guidelines for meditation if you have never meditated before:

1. Consistency: the most important part of effective meditation is consistency. When you are beginning with a completely untrained mind, you have to begin with what regulations you can so that your untrained mind gets used to the new way you are using it. Meditate at the same time each day, for the same length of time (preferably in the same place each time).

   This sort of external consistency will help your mind make the transition into meditation more easily. You can pick any time of the day that works best for you, just so long as you do it at that same time each day. One good trick for beginners is to practice meditating immediately before bed. Some people find themselves getting impatient when they first start trying meditation. So if you practice before bed, this will decrease the impatience because there isn't anything else you could be doing instead. You might as well use that time before you fall asleep to meditate since you would otherwise not use it for anything (or worse, you would use that time to worry about the stresses in your life which is counterproductive).

2. Pace yourself: if you are a complete beginner to meditation, don't get over ambitious. Commit to just 2 minutes of meditation per day at the beginning. That may sound like nothing but when you are just starting out, two minutes is more than enough to start getting your mind acquainted with the process. Set a time for yourself so that you don't have to think about the time at all while you are meditating.

Once you find that you feel like the 2 minute timer is interrupting your relaxation, extend it to 5 minutes. Eventually, you won't need to use any kind of timer at all. You can simply meditate for as long as you feel like meditating. But in the beginning, the timer will be useful.

Another advantage to starting with just 2 minutes per day is that it will be extremely easy for you to find 2 minutes somewhere in your schedule to practice meditation. You won't feel burdened by the responsibility of having to meditate. It will be quick, easy, and something you might find yourself even looking forward to.

3. Find your space: choose a place to do your meditation. You want to try and use the same space every single time you meditate so pick somewhere convenient. It can be as simple as a quiet room in the house or even in the bathroom while you take a bath. It could also be a calm, secluded area in a nearby park if you want the added benefit of nature's relaxing qualities.

The key is to choose some quiet, relaxing, and easy for you to get to location on a daily basis so that you can use this same exact spot each and every time. Your mind and body will soon begin to associate this location with the act of meditation so that as soon as you sit down, your mind is already getting prepared for the task.

4. Get comfortable: Just as you want a calm and relaxing location, you also need to have a posture and clothing which are relaxing. If you sit slouched over, your back will eventually begin to hurt. If you wear tight, restrictive clothing, it will be hard for you to focus on anything other than the discomfort. You want to minimize physical sensations as much as possible. As you become better trained in meditation, you will be able to overcome physical sensations more easily but in the beginning, even the slightest discomfort can be a serious distraction and prevent

you from fully clearing your mind as is required with meditation.

5. Focus on your breathing: to help clear your mind, you should try focusing on one simple, repetitive act. Breathing is the best choice for this. Let all of the other thoughts (positive, negative, or otherwise) drain out of your mind as you become entirely focused on the act of breathing. Repeat a mantra as you do this. A mantra is a single sound, word, or phrase that you repeat over and over in order to help clear the thoughts from your mind.

To help regulate your breathing you can choose a mantra like "Inhale. $1 - 2 - 3$. Exhale. $1 -2 -3$" or something along those lines. You want to breathe slowly, allowing each breath to fill every single corner of your lungs and expand your chest to its fullest extent. Then, you want to exhale slowly making sure to clear out all the space in your chest and lungs.

Focus on every physical sensation of your breath, the way your chest feels as it stretches outward; the way your nose and throat feel as the air is passing through; the way your head and neck become lighter; and so on. And with each exhalation, imagine that your thoughts are being released along with your breath and carried away on the wind.

<u>Affirmation</u>

Affirmations are a key part of creative visualization as well as an excellent way to help increase your mental strength. The express purpose of affirmation is to increase positive thoughts and decrease negative thoughts. It can also help you improve your focus to a certain extent but this is not its primary task. Essentially, affirmations are specific positive thoughts that you make ahead of time and then use to train your brain in order to think positively.

Affirmations are commonly used as a standalone technique in therapy for helping people overcome depression, anxiety, or phobias. However, in conjunction with creative visualization, they are most often geared toward the goals or achievements you are trying to attain with your creative visualization. In either case, there are a few simple guidelines for making sure that your affirmations are effective:

- Positive statements: in order to be a true affirmation, you have to use a positive thought. At first glance, you might be thinking "well, obviously." But this means more than just good or beneficial thinking. In this case, positive thought means a statement that does not contain a single negative word. For example, telling yourself "I will not drink soda" might sound like a positive thought since the meaning of it is positive (not drinking unhealthy soda). However, this statement is actually negative because the statement requires an absence. Rather than filling your life with something positive, you are simply removing something negative.

A positive affirmation for someone who wants to quit drinking soda would be something like "I drink water instead of soda" or "I drink tea instead of soda." The important thing here is that the statement contains no negative words and that it be said in the present tense. An affirmation that says "I will" will never come true because it is always referring to a future point that you haven't yet reached. Instead, the affirmation should be phrased as if this is something you *already* do. You don't *want* to quit drinking soda, you *did* quit drinking soda.

- Simplified phrases: the simpler the sentence is, the more effective it will be. You don't want to have to repeat a Shakespearean soliloquy to yourself each morning, do you? The point of the affirmation is to be something quick that you can remember easily and repeat multiple times. If you have seen the film Inception, you know that in order for an idea to penetrate your subconscious, it must be as simplified as possible.

If the goal you are trying to achieve through creative visualization is too complex to boil down into a simple affirmation, try breaking it down into a set of multiple, simple affirmations. For example, if you are visualizing yourself as wealthy, successful, and living somewhere beautiful, come up with a separate affirmation for each element of your visualization.

- Frequent repetition: in order for affirmations to work, you cannot just tell it to yourself one time. You need to repeat it multiple times throughout the day, every single day. Try to make a habit of it. As soon as you wake up in the morning, before you have even gotten out of bed, repeat your affirmations to yourself. Repeat them again as you are falling asleep at night.

These two times of day (right when waking up and right before falling asleep) are the ideal times to repeat your affirmations. This is because the barrier between your conscious and subconscious mind is at its weakest during these times and therefore your subconscious will be more receptive to the thoughts your conscious mind is making. Therefore, it will be easier for these affirmations to become deeply rooted in your mind and help influence the shape of your unconscious feelings and desires.

<u>Release</u>

You should practice release even when you become more highly trained in the techniques of creative visualization. However, it is even more important at the beginning when your mind is still more or less untrained. Release is the art of letting go of your negative thoughts. To do so effectively requires a few steps.

First of all, as soon as a negative thought pops into your mind, stop and take a moment to analyze that thought. What was it that triggered the negative thought? What is it that makes you believe this thought is true? What are the unconscious fears and anxieties that are hidden beneath it?

Let's try an example. Say that you have the negative thought "I will never earn enough money." Stop and analyze this. What sort of fears and anxieties are underneath this statement? Did you grow up relatively poor or financially strained? Have you recently experienced some sort of significant loss?

The process of thoroughly understanding where these negative thoughts are coming from will help you to effectively eliminate them. You will be able to recognize the false beliefs that have led you to think the negative thoughts are true.

The next time this same negative thought occurs, stop the thought and replace it with a positive affirmation. You can use one of the affirmations you are already using for the creative visualization process or you can make a new affirmation that is specifically designed to counteract the negative thought. In the case of "I will never earn enough money", for example, you could counteract it with an affirmation like "I have more money than my parents had" or "I earn enough money to meet my financial obligations."

This is going to be a difficult process at first since these negative thoughts have become so deeply rooted in your mind already but the more you work at it, the less rooted they will become and eventually you will be able to eliminate them entirely.

Acceptance

Another method of improving your mental strength is to practice acceptance. Acceptance refers to learning to recognize the parts of your life which are out of your control and cultivating the ability to go with the flow. For example, you might often encounter traffic during your commute to work. This can be extremely frustrating and stressful because it is slowing you down.

Recognize that you cannot control the traffic. Rather than become frustrated, leave a bit earlier for work so that you know that even with the traffic, you will get to work on time. And once you understand that you can get to work on time even in traffic, let go of those negative feelings of frustration and impatience. Accept the traffic and use that time constructively. Repeat your affirmations to yourself, listen to an audio book, think constructively about some of the problems you *can* control.

When you practice acceptance, you can learn to see even these negative aspects of your life as something positive or at least constructive. You can learn to appreciate that extra time you have for yourself during the traffic because you have learned to use that time to improve yourself.

<u>Endurance</u>

Mental endurance is a great skill to practice. This refers to the ability to tolerate inconvenience and discomfort. When doing a task you do not enjoy like cleaning the dishes or mowing the lawn, rather than focusing on how tedious or unpleasant it is, practice tolerance. Remind yourself that while this is tedious, if you focus on the details of doing the task correctly and absorbing the unpleasantness, it will soon be over and out of the way entirely.

The higher your endurance becomes, the less troublesome your responsibilities and obligations will be. You can complete even the task you dislike without becoming stressed or anxious. And then, once they are over, you will know that it is done and you can move on to something else, putting it out of your mind entirely.

Get Out of Your Comfort Zone

As humans, we have a tendency to build up routines and become more or less comfortable in our way of life even if that way of life does not necessarily make us happy. This is because, at the unconscious level, we are afraid of taking risks. We fear that, even though we are not happy now, the alternative could end up making us far unhappier than we were before.

But if you are afraid to take risks, you are going to be too timid to seize the opportunities that the universe is trying to send to you. And you might miss out on the chance to expose yourself to even more opportunities.

To counteract this habit of sticking to your comfort zone, break out of it every chance you get, even if it is only in small ways. This can be as minor as trying out new recipes throughout the week rather than eating the same old meals you always eat. When you go out on the weekend, go somewhere you haven't gone before. If there is something you have always wanted to try but always felt a little too timid to actually do it, try it!

Take a dance lesson. Join a language course. Try the weirdest thing on the menu. Just do anything you can to make yourself more comfortable with being outside of your comfort zone. You might be surprised what you discover about yourself and the world around you!

Common Mistakes People Make

While you are working at these techniques and methods, you can make the work a lot easier on yourself if you avoid these all too common mistakes. The methods you just read about are actually designed to help counteract these mistakes but it is better that you are consciously aware of them so that you are better prepared to resist making them yourself:

Lack of belief

As mentioned earlier, doubt can be very harmful to the effectiveness of your creative visualization. Doubt emits negative vibrations just as visualization emits positive ones. Work on building a strong foundation of belief in the methods and techniques. With this foundation, the techniques will not only be more effective but you will be more motivated to put in the effort and dedication they require to work.

<u>Giving up too early</u>

This is probably the most common mistake people make. Creative visualization takes patience and, more so, it takes the ability to recognize when it is working. Many people try creative visualization for a couple of days and then when millions of dollars don't immediately drop into their lap, they give up on it. You have to stick with this for awhile, keep putting out more and more positive vibrations into the universe and then use the positive reflection technique you read about above in order to recognize the opportunities and positivity that the universe is sending your way in response to your creative visualization.

Using the future tense

As you read in the section about affirmations, you should not be thinking in the future tense. Creative visualization should be done in the present tense. Don't imagine that you *will be* wealthy some day, visualize yourself as wealthy right now. Think in terms of the present and what you are going to do *today* to make your dreams come true.

Being too cautious

If you are too afraid to take risks, you are going to prevent yourself from ever achieving your goals no matter how much you use creative visualization. The universe isn't just going to drop money or success into your lap. It is going to provide you with opportunities to do it yourself. This means you have to be ready for the risks that come with those opportunities. No successful person on this planet achieved success by choosing the easiest path or the safest path. They took risks, they ventured into the unknown, they abandoned their comfort zones to go into entirely unfamiliar territory and seize the opportunities they found there.

Chapter 4: What is Self Hypnosis?

Self hypnosis (also known as autohypnosis) is the process of hypnotizing yourself. In hypnotizing yourself, your mind becomes more open to suggestion and you can make self suggestions (or "autosuggestions") to help alter your behavior, beliefs, or emotions.

In film, hypnosis is often portrayed negatively as a device for exercising mind control and manipulation of others. It is usually shown in extremes where the person under hypnosis is made to commit some horrendous act and then later has no memory of it. However, in reality, the effects of hypnosis are much different. It does not brainwash you or control your mind. Rather, it is a method of directly accessing your unconscious mind. However, you are still aware and in control of yourself and come out of the hypnotic state whenever you wish.

Psychiatrists often use traditional hypnosis in order to open the patient's unconscious mind and better understand it without having to break past the often rigid barriers put in place by the conscious mind. The psychiatrist cannot then make you do things you would not want to do. Instead, he or she is simply putting you into a state in which it is possible to talk directly with your unconscious mind.

Self hypnosis is also widely used in therapy to help patients in between these therapeutic sessions so that they can deeply internalize the therapeutic advice of their psychiatrist or therapist. However, it is now becoming more common even outside of therapy as a self improvement method that helps you make the important changes you want to make in your life.

Unlike creative visualization, self hypnosis is more often used for internal changes rather than external changes. If you want to achieve wealth and success, use creative visualization. If you want to lose weight or quit smoking, use self hypnosis.

Hypnotism was first developed in the 19th century by a Scottish surgeon named James Braid. Two years after developing hypnotism, he developed techniques for self hypnosis. He taught the techniques to many of his clients and also used it regularly on himself.

In the 20th century, Emile Coue recognized the immense potential that lay within self hypnosis and created a self improvement system that soon became internationally famous. A German psychiatrist furthered these methods into what he referred to as "autogenic training" which used a very specific step by step process in order to retrain your mind to overcome various psychological and emotional disorders.

Since the 1930s, much research has been done on self hypnosis (generally from the perspective of psychiatry) to better understand how and why it works as well as how effective it really is.

Recent research has revealed that it is as effective as traditional hypnosis (in which another person hypnotizes you).

An alternative way of understanding self hypnosis is to think of it in terms of the alternate name that James Braid (the original developer of the method) gave it: monoideaism. The first part of this word, "mono", means one or single. The second part refers to idea. Therefore, self hypnosis is a means of intensifying your focus into a single direction or thought. In this heightened mental state, your focus is extremely sharpened and your mind becomes more open to suggestions. This is also often accompanied by a state of relaxation (this is not always the case, however).

In everyday terms, you can compare self hypnosis in some ways to day dreaming. While day dreaming is less focused or guided, it shares some similar characteristics with self hypnosis. Your mind becomes fixed on a single idea or scene; you are less aware of your surroundings;

and you are sometimes in a more relaxed state, or at least less aware of any physical or emotional discomfort. Yet, even in this state, you still maintain in full control and are able to "snap out of it" whenever you choose.

Chapter 5: The Benefits of Self-Hypnosis

Self hypnosis can be used to accomplish many things and is actually a surprisingly powerful and useful technique. Mastering it will give you another powerful tool in your mental toolbox to help you take control of yourself and your life. It is extremely effective in promoting healthy changes to your emotions, attitudes, and habits but it can also be used as a treatment method for various issues. The following is a short list of some of the things self hypnosis is commonly used for:

- Stress management: self hypnosis is a great tool for managing your stress. Not only does the relaxed state often achieved with self hypnosis help lower stress immediately but in the long term, your stress levels will remain lower than usual. This is because the method helps provide you with greater control over your emotions and how you react to external stimuli.

Stress typically represents a lack of control. It starts with feeling as if you cannot control the situation which is causing stress and then continues with an inability to control the anxiety and worry you feel regarding the situation. With self hypnosis, you can regain control and train your mind to respond to stressful situations with less anxiety and panic.

- Weight loss: it can also be used to help you lose weight. No, it's not some magic technique where you hypnotize the excess fat into leaving your body. Rather, it works by retraining your habits and giving you greater control over your hunger, cravings, and taste.

You can use self hypnosis to lower your appetite throughout the day or to feel full for a longer period of time after a meal.

This is because both feelings of "fullness" and "hunger" are actually triggered by your mind, not your stomach. This is why you can still eat even when you are physically full and why you can feel repelled by food even when your stomach is physically empty. With self hypnosis, you can better control the signal your mind sends to your stomach so that you can regulate your appetite and eat less.

- Improve health: it has been used in the treatment of all sorts of illnesses from skin conditions to asthma. This is because many illnesses have physiological components (that is, they are physical conditions but can be triggered or made worse by your particular psychological or emotional state). In gaining a better handle of your psychological state, you can better manage the physical illness as well.

For example, an asthma attack can be triggered by the sudden onset of panic. If you can better control your mental state so that you do not become easily panicked, you will minimize the number of asthmatic attacks you have.

- Quit smoking: self hypnosis is actually a very popular method used to help people quit smoking. With this method, you can actually minimize your cravings for nicotine and manage the physical side effects of withdrawal. Essentially, you are retraining your mind to become the mind of a nonsmoker.

- Change your habits: just as it is used to help people quit smoking or to lose weight, self hypnosis can be used to get rid of or to cultivate just about any personal habit you can think of. It is a great method for retraining your mind and planting the seeds in your unconscious to begin doing (or stop doing) something.

- Save money: you can even use self hypnosis to help you save money by budgeting better and spending less. Through self hypnosis, you can retrain yourself to not give into impulses or make compulsive purchases when you are at the store. It can help you stay focused so that you can go into a store, get exactly what you came for and nothing else.

You can also use self hypnosis to retrain yourself to want less material possessions. If you have a serious thing for shoes or purses, you can use self hypnosis to decrease your obsession with them. That doesn't mean you will hate them or stop buying them, it just means you won't feel the need to buy every cute pair of shoes you see and it can help you feel more satisfied with the things you already own.

- Overcome emotional distress: this is one of the classic uses of self hypnosis as well as traditional hypnosis. As you read in chapter 4, psychiatrists have been researching the potential uses of self hypnosis as a therapeutic method for more than a century and rely upon it more and more as an effective technique for helping patients process their emotions and overcome past trauma.

- Recover from treatment: it is also widely used after surgery or other medical treatments to help heal more quickly as well as decrease your need for post treatment medications like pain killers and such. Your mind sends the signals to your body that tell it to heal. If you practice self hypnosis, you can actually intensify these signals and help your body to heal faster.

- Eat healthier: as mentioned earlier regarding weight loss, this method can help you change your eating habits. But it can do more than control your appetite and cravings. It can even change the foods you like. If you find yourself eating way too many sweets and not enough vegetables, you can actually reprogram your mind to be less attracted to sweets and to crave the flavor of vegetables.

While our taste buds are responsible for detecting the taste of food, it is actually our brain that is responsible for forming our reaction to those tastes. That is, if there is a vegetable you don't like, it really doesn't have anything to do with the actual taste of the vegetable. It has to do with the signals your brain sends in response to that taste. With self hypnosis, you can change those signals and teach yourself to enjoy the taste of healthy foods. This is way more effective than any diet.

- Exercise more: self hypnosis can also be a source of motivation. When you are working at the subconscious level as you are with this method, you are changing your fundamental attitude toward the things around you. If you have always planned to start exercising more but never seemed able to get up the energy to actually go and do it, self hypnosis can create that energy in your very core and turn you into a person who not only exercises regularly but actually looks forward to exercising.

- Pain management: this method is widely used for pain management. This is because the intensified focus involved in self hypnosis allows you to direct your mind away from the pain you feel. If your brain is not at all focused on the pain, you will not feel it at all. This is because, as with many other physical processes, pain is a function of the mind.

The nervous system throughout your body which is responsible for detecting pain signals (such as when you get cut, burned, or have sore muscles) is controlled by your brain. The nerves send a signal to your brain and then your brain returns a signal which instructs the nerve to feel pain. However, if your brain is focused in the act of self hypnosis, it will be too preoccupied to respond to the signals your nerve is sending. The pain will literally disappear because your brain is no longer telling your body to feel it.

- Sleep disorders: when you become highly trained in self hypnosis, you will actually have the ability to fall asleep instantaneously as soon as you want to (you can do the same with waking up). This means no more lying around in bed waiting to finally fall asleep. That is a high level of mastery, however. But even at lower levels of skill, you will be able to fall asleep more quickly. And the more you practice self hypnosis for this purpose, the better you will get at controlling your sleep patterns so that you can take charge of your schedule and feel more alert throughout the day.

- Improve cognitive skills: self hypnosis can even be used to help improve many important cognitive skills. You can use it to improve your memory, concentration, focus, or problem solving skills. So if you have troubles with any of these or simply would like to perfect them, self hypnosis is one of the best methods of doing so.

Chapter 6: Strategies for Effective Self Hypnosis

If you have a very specific purpose for using self hypnosis (such as training a specific habit, quitting smoking, losing weight, eating healthier, and so on) then it is recommended that you buy a specific course for using self hypnosis in order to accomplish that specific goal. There are many books and audio courses out there to help you apply the techniques of self hypnosis to the specific goals you have in mind.

For the less specific tasks (such as pain management, recovering from emotional distress, reducing stress, and so on) you can follow the general steps described below:

1. Get comfortable: wear comfortable clothing that does not pinch or pull anywhere. Pajamas or workout clothes are ideal for this. Or, if you are the type to feel

more comfortable in no clothing, you can even do this naked or in your underwear! The important thing is that you are as comfortable as possible so that there are no physical sensations distracting you from the task at hand.

2. Find a good location: find a relaxing space in which you will have no distractions. There should be a comfortable place to sit or lie down. It should be quiet and relatively secluded (at least for the time in which you will be using it for hypnosis). Use this same location each time that you do self-hypnosis.

3. Remove all distractions: turn off your cell phone. That is, turn it completely off! Do not just silence it. Turn off the television, the radio, the computer, and any other electronics. Lock the door if possible. Close the blinds on the window. Try to

make this space completely cut off from the external world in every way possible.

4. Identify your goals: before you start the process of self hypnosis, you should identify what your goals are with self hypnosis. They don't have to be so specific. It could be as general as "I want to be more confident" or "I want to sleep better." Create positive affirmations for these goals according to the instructions you read about in chapter 3. You will be using these later so it is important that you have them ready before you begin self hypnosis.

5. Find a point of concentration: choose a point, any point at all, and focus on it. It could be the corner of a picture frame, a stain on the wall, a letter in the title on the spine of a book. It can be anything at all so long as it doesn't move. Alternatively, you can close your eyes and focus on your

own eyelids as a point of concentration. This is the best choice if you feel that you will have a hard time holding your gaze on one single spot in the room.

6. Start clearing your mind: begin to release feelings of anxiety and worry. Give yourself over to the feeling of relaxation. Enjoy the comfortable clothing you are in, the tranquil quiet space you have created for yourself. Allow yourself to focus on this present moment rather than past or future worries.

   You can move on to the next steps even before you feel that all your worries have disappeared. In fact, move on to the next step as soon as you start to feel that process beginning. Anxiety will continue to disappear as you move through the other steps so don't feel pressure to eliminate it all at once.

7. Become aware of your body: start to feel the tension in your body parts release. Begin with your toes, then the balls of your feet, then the heels, then the ankles, and continue moving up, part by part, feeling the tension get released and the muscles become relaxed.

8. Focus on your breathing: take long, deep slow breaths. You can do this at the same time that you are becoming aware of your body. With each inhalation, become focused on a new part of the body. And with each exhalation, allow that part of your body to release all of its tension.

9. Visualize a simple, relaxing scene: this does not have to be an idyllic natural scene or your dream vacation. In fact, it should be much more simplified. The important elements are that the scene is dark, warm, and gentle. One predesigned scene many people use is a dark basement

filled with warm water that they can swim in. Whatever your scene is, you are just visualizing it right now. Do not visualize yourself in this scene yet.

10. Move toward that scene: now, move step by step toward that scene. In the example of the basement, there will be steps leading down into the water. The water level will come up to about halfway on the staircase so that your feet are already in the water at this halfway point and you become further and further submerged with each step you take until you are swimming. Make as many steps as you want. If this is one of your first time doing self hypnosis, you should add more steps (try starting with around 30 steps with the 15th step being the halfway point at which your feet touch the water).

11. Feel the floating sensation: by the time you have become submerged in the water,

you should feel a sort of floating sensation. Your body's tension is fully released and you are completely immersed in the experience of the scene you have visualized and now in. If you do not feel this floating sensation, repeat step 10 over again. It is alright if you don't master this feeling the first time, don't feel pressured to attain this feeling. The important thing is that you appreciate every sensation of every step along the way. Focus entirely on completing each step with no thought to the step that comes next nor the step that came before.

12. Narrate your experience: describe what you feel, what you see, and what you do. You can do this out loud or in your head. But clearly tell yourself things like "I feel that I am floating" or "I can see the gentle ripples in the water" and so on. Allow objects to appear in the water. They can be boxes, bottles, or any other kind of

container that you prefer. Swim toward them. Remember to narrate all of this to yourself.

13. Repeat your affirmations: each of those containers holds one of your affirmations, as you swim toward one and open it, repeat one of your affirmations. Repeat this process with each container in the water. Narrate the feeling as you open each one and the feeling after you repeat your affirmation.

14. Slowly exit hypnosis: to leave this hypnotic state, go back the way you came. Swim toward the stairs and begin taking the stairs slowly back up, out of the water. Counting each one along the way. Do it as slowly as possible, you do not want to rush yourself. Feel the water leaving and your skin drying off in the warm air.

Conclusion

With the strategies in this book, you are ready to start using creative visualization and self hypnosis today! You already have the only tool you will ever need: your mind. Keep this book on hand so that you can refer to it whenever you need to refresh your memory about the specific techniques and methods you should be practicing.

You can also keep it as a source of inspiration whenever you start feeling that doubts or negativity are starting to creep back into your mind. Read through the benefits chapters again to remind yourself of all the amazing benefits that you are already experiencing *and* the even more amazing benefits that you will have in the future!

Practice these techniques every single day and pick the methods that appeal to you the most so that you can help your mind grow stronger even more quickly. Commit to it for at least one hour per day (you can split this up into 2 or 3 different sessions). If you can find more time for it, that would be even better.

Now that you have finished reading, you are ready to start making your life better by achieving success and becoming exactly the person you have always dreamed of being. Start today by deciding exactly what it is you truly desire and then start following the steps to visualize it properly.

Good luck on your journey and may you find all the happiness and success that you desire. Because you deserve it!

Other books available by author on Kindle, Paperback and Audio

Manifesting Abundance: The Secret Principles Of Using The Law Of Attraction To Manifest Wealth, Love, Happiness And Anything You Can Imagine

Manufactured by Amazon.ca
Bolton, ON

12151347R00053